Images From Hell

by

F.L. Riker

Bloomington, IN  Milton Keynes, UK

authorHOUSE®

AuthorHouse™
1663 Liberty Drive, Suite 200
Bloomington, IN 47403
www.authorhouse.com
Phone: 1-800-839-8640

AuthorHouse™ UK Ltd.
500 Avebury Boulevard
Central Milton Keynes, MK9 2BE
www.authorhouse.co.uk
Phone: 08001974150

First published by AuthorHouse 7/18/2006

ISBN: 1-4208-4285-4 (sc)

Library of Congress Control Number: 2005902587

Printed in the United States of America
Bloomington, Indiana

This book is printed on acid-free paper.

TABLE OF CONTENTS

THE GAME

Isolation is the absence of insanity

Insanity is the cure for isolation

THIS LAND

Shame or guilt, no I felt nothing when she dropped
I was cold in the heart, didn't want to be stopped
Killing everything that moved, I was insane at the time
Everything was legal; there was no such thing as crime.

The guy next to me had his hand shot off
I fired with reflex, anger and confusion
I wanted to kill, that's all that mattered
Killing was my only job there was no delusion.

The girl on the bike was only twelve
The round of bullets went through her chest
She could have been the sniper that took my friend's hand
I had no regrets I felt I did my best.

The sniper had stopped when the girl was killed
My little burst was about all it took
Maybe I was right, no one would ever know
The war just went on, no one gave me a look.

I was promoted that day to lead all my friends
A promotion for killing a little girl on a bike
That was the name of the game in this war torn land
A rifle she held across her back, it was her that did the strike.

The little kids are running this war

Ten year olds walking up with grenades in their bags

Twelve year olds firing rifles at night

During the day they wore civilian rags.

Killing and bloodshed on every corner you come to

This is a horrid place to be, it'll drive you insane

The dead, the dying, the bleeding from the heart

Just thinking about all the blood, and more and more of the same.

MY FIRST

Napalm it was, the true fires of hell

Woman and children caught in the midst

Breathing the oven that came from the sky

The village, the people, all cease to exist

My eyes burned from the heat, couldn't believe

Hearing the screams, the cries, the torture I see

My first taste of war in a horrible land

There was no emotion, stone cold, no longer me

From that day I was hard in my heart

My eyes were cold, didn't care anymore

The dark burning flesh went deep within me

My mind, no escape, the black peeling flesh had closed the door

A soldier now and anxious to kill

No feeling at all, save the hate and confusion

I had the blank empty stare of many others I saw

Any God there was, now just an illusion

ONE FIGHT

I'm wounded; I'm down, in and out of blackness
The fight is still going but too scared to move
On and off, totally blinded, still clutching my weapon
We were the good guys, no way could we lose.

I felt hands on me, someone grabbed at my rifle
I was still in the fight, I fired at will
Not thinking, not seeing, just instant frustration
Only one thing going in my brain, kill, just fire and kill.

I opened my eyes for an instant and looked to the side
The man I had shot was someone I knew
My eyes closed again not able to think
I expected to die now to pay back what's due.

There were dozens of Cong already inside
Hundreds more just waiting to kill us all
I couldn't do anything to help my friends
Back into blackness, I just didn't care who would fall.

By light it was over, I started to move
Total blackness surrounding my head
All I could do was lay there and feel hands around me
I feel more pain now and sore all over, I'd much rather have been
dead instead.

SAVAGE COUNTRY

Teary eyes and burning mind among the shadows of the night,
The darkness bleeding into my heart too fast to control.
All the bitter memories possess my soul to overloading,
I'm filled to the top with what my brain no longer needs to know.

Scared? Oh yes! They're coming in waves,
The enemy is here now I know it's time to die.
Blood dripping madness is now taking over,
Holes in my flesh, blood on my face and here I lie.

Now I can hear the birds far off in the distance,
Don't take me out - I'm not yet dead.
I missed most of the fight, feel guilt and shame,
Others help me up to the birds, then the pain in my head!

It surrounds me that pain, I don't know what hit me,
Blood all over from me and all the others.
I sit on the chopper looking down at the madness,
Bodies not moving some under cover.

The guy on the stretcher is a very good friend,
I'm not so bad, I now feel more shame.
Laying face down, huge metal in his back,
The dead, the guts all over, I can't remember his name.

This fight is over, my friend passed away,

I remember his name now and the other dead.

They stitched me up and sent me back; here I have to stay,

I guess I'll live for another fight, remembering the blood I shed.

ISOLATION

Isolation was the key to survival for someone like me
Mind far distant from known reality
Scared and afraid of every sound I heard
Hiding my soul from the world was me.

My heart bleeds black, my eyes bleed red
Nothing made sense in the world I was in
Crouching in corners afraid of the night
People surrounding me got under my skin.

I had the infection deep down inside
Nothing could bring me out of my shell
I felt shame and hurt that no one else had
Alone in the darkness to fend for myself.

Not talking to a soul, show no emotion at all
Take long walks at night hoping for death
Take risk intentionally just to prove I'm alive
Live or die meant nothing was the burning in my soul.

When I tried to get help they blanketed me
Too many people digging at my past
Making me talk about it made me insane
That thing in me will always last.

Isolation was the only cure

I stayed to myself never muttering a word

I couldn't talk about it, no, no more

Isolation, the absence of insanity is what they heard.

I knew I would panic if this kept on

Hiding under bridges was a solid way of life

I slept on railroad tracks in the dead of night

I drank myself to the floor with memories so rife.

No one could understand, alone in my cage

There was no one to hear the cry's I made

It was tormenting, this evil thing

Nightmares filled my every blink then another raid.

Back under a bridge to fight my fears

I deserted my family in my time of need

They'd never understand, no one could

This insane war had planted its seed.

THE EFFECT OF WAR

Who made this vessel of humanity?
Truly the ship of a fool with fatal flaws so rife
Who made the weakness and impotence I am
He who dares to call me life

I challenge this maker of defective ware
A challenge to he who developed this broken shell
To heal the mind of this tortured soul
To amend his mistakes or send me to hell

The challenge is in, the dare is put forth
Repair this life of agonizing pain
For now I no longer see the path ahead
I pause, I waiver, I stand here insane

Now to hear the verdict of so many years
The sentence to finally be passed
As payment for all the life I've led
Death, forever and a day they asked

The pain seems subsiding, a relaxing air
It's all so easy to comprehend
Envisions of peace are filling my mind
And now this life must end.

DURATION

In these closed dark spaces of my mind

I feel the deepening horror,

Digging blood dripping pitchforks

Torture me throughout my whole,

Empty blackened walls they now surround me

Reaching hopelessly for a single blood soaked door,

In this dreadful while of time

I'll now spend with the devil in my soul

Never ending hell is all that's left for me

Nothing left of the world I knew

From now I'll never see.

A VICTIM

Now hiding in the massive crowd
People moving through my empty stare
They see no one where I am
I don't exist or they just don't care.

I hold daggers in my eyes and fear in my damaged soul
The meaning of life has abandoned me
These people are trampling on my cold torn heart
The war still in me but they just can't see.

Still hiding from the gnawing fingers of death
In a crowd is the easiest way to escape
No one sees me, no one cares, and no one speaks my way
I hold it in my mind; my mind is the victim of rape.

I'm one of the victims of a crazy time
I walk around empty maybe going insane
I feel the heartbeats of only the dead
I see the ghosts in front of me then comes the pain.

IN ME

I'm lost in a dimension I can't understand

Bloody heads bobbing in a vast sea of fire

Some young, some old, most don't belong here

My nightmare, my horror, the Gods all seem to conspire

I waken to sweating, sometimes a scream

I didn't do this, why am I here?

Above all the fire, a blood dripping sword

It's in me at night, the heart pounding fear

I can't understand, I tremble in terror

It seems so alive, but not part of me

Is it in me, the devil? My future unfolding

In the dark, in the night, it's all I can see

I seem all alone in this dark hellish realm

Alone with the fear and the blood of so many

I can't make it stop, it's there every night

In my mind I search for reason, but find not any

Confused and tortured to the point of insane

Afraid to sleep, afraid of the night

Exhaustion reigns, can't find my way out

Freedom is somewhere, but in my fear, I've lost site

ALONE

No one to talk to, no one to hold or touch.

No one to whom I can whisper the inner cries of my heart.

Help me, I'm alone here.

Always alone. No one near. No one to hear.

I shake with horrid screams of the burning children.

I see their flesh peeling a black and bloody mix of grotesque pain.

I'm the only one here. The only one to hear.

What words could there ever be?

Alone, always alone.

If time stops at death, then too, future, motion, progression.

For an eternity, nothing, save the last second of shear horror.

The burning horror of life itself.

Alone, always alone.

We each die alone. Perhaps as we've lived.

No one to hear the cry. No one to share the pain of simply being alone.

Always alone.

I need to be touched. I crave wildly for affection, for someone to

care, someone to love me.

The fear of dying alone. I search and I cry, always in vain.

Alone, always alone.

I suffer with the children. No one to embrace them

No one to hear their needs. No one left to care.

They died alone. Each alone. Forever alone. As I.

Only the sounds of being alone for the eternity of one.

No one will hear. No one will care.

Not even a tiny memory of a ripple in the ocean

There's no one there. No one here.

I live here lonelier than my heart should allow.

Time has stopped for me. I feel nothing but the agony and pain of

being alone.

Truly alone. The horror of life, to be alone, forever alone.

I can no longer see tomorrow. Only the pain of yesterday.

Time has stopped there. What words are there?

What hopes are left? Time is gone.

Empty thoughts. Lost dreams. No longer life. No progression.

No future. Only the hurt of today.

I've stopped with time now.

I'll go see the children. I can embrace the lost loves.

Or will there be only today? Only now? Only the hurt?

Alone. Forever alone.

THUNDER

Thunder is a common occurrence, especially in the mind,
The lightning bolts are painful, torture for all mankind,
Especially the soldier who has put his life on the line,
The lives he took, the blood he shed, only to be left behind.

Is it any wonder that we cry now for our sins,
Taking another life can't be justified in our brains,
Try to stop the bleeding of all those wounded friends,
Then you'll realize, his life will be taken before his gains.

We gave up so much, even to insanity,
The loneliness we feel, the heartaches plague us still,
Death has been through our doors now, just too many times,
The blood we still see, the nightmares against our will.

I've done my share and I hate my sins,
My mind isn't the same; I relinquished my soul to tears,
The thunder in my mind, it seems it always wins,
The lightning in my heart passes along all new fears.

I've known so many who went to suicide,
The rest of us are all still trying to hide,
Cover it up, that's the name of the game,
In my heart and my soul I feel so much shame.

Then I found a wife who really understands,

I share it with her, she lightens the enormous strain,

A beautiful compromise is calming the soul,

The thunder is stopping, for I've paid the toll.

DEATH OF A CAPTIVE

I stand alone in my little portion of insanity

My mind flickering in all directions

My soul is in turmoil, my heart beats sporadic

I feel nothing but the pain of captivity.

I must survive the dreadful pain

If only to see what my heart has missed

The wonders, the beauty, all just a dream

In this aloneness, I feel condemned to drift inane.

My eyes are blind, my brain is weary

Nothing of the former self exist

Alone in a universe of confusion

Alone, to feel all this pain so severely.

I may come out of this, I may survive

But at this point I don't see why

The pain would be with me forever,

And sooner, rather than later, I'll die.

COMPLAISANT DEATH

My head is filled with darkness
So very few thoughts running through
No way out of this eternal blackness
There is no light, nothing I can do.

This feeling has been with me a very long time
Since the war I've been a living dead
My mind just went, no feelings at all
I'm cold and lonely, only pain in my head.

All these years I've been in wonder
Is there nothing beyond this freezer of fear?
If I die it will be a complaisant death
Then I'm alone; no one will shed a tear.

Death itself is a way of life
We're set up to repeat all our sins
From beginning to end and then all over again
The dead feel more pain, nobody wins.

Sometimes I don't want to die; sometimes I wish I were dead
All the time I'm confused, is this all in my head?
Sometimes I feel I'm already gone
Most of the time I know I am.

The blackness is really getting to me

This is certainly the end

I could do it myself, but I pause and I shake

Where is there someone to help me see.

ILLEGAL MEMORIES

The memories I have are against the law
My mind is burning with secrets of long ago
The killing, the maiming, everything I saw
These memories I have in me will certainly last.

The torture, the demons, the dogs of war
All in my head for only me to see
I can't talk to you about any of this
But my mind is in torture, I can't be me.

What other people see is just a front
What I see in myself will imprison me forever
They'll get me one day, it won't be long
My long sought hope will come to me never.

If I mention this, they'll take me down to the hanging tree
Where I'll go to hell and never be forgiven
There were others with me through all of this
I'll go along with the rest and never be free.

It's holding me, these illegal memories
Binding my heart and soul through eternity
Never seeing life, just tears and fears
Just drifting through hell, for this is the real me.

21

I'm timid, I'm weak, I couldn't take all of that

The pain and the blood tore me apart

All these memories I've had for years

I finish this poem with agony in my heart.

VICTIMS INN

I look at the prizes of war, on just another empty wall
I feel the pressure still, that keeps on clamping my heart
I'm blinded by the obscene darkness of it all
I feel the emptiness and total loss that crept in slowly from the start.

Was it worth the losses I had to endure
My walls are void of family and friends
In my little room of darkness are nothing but the victims
Haunting in blackness, devouring my worth to all the ends.

A whole new realm of persisting emptiness covers my soul
The war left no feeling save the agony of the victims' blood
The sights, the smells, the morbid piles of open flesh
Draining every cell from me with a staunch emotional flood.

There seems nothing left of my being as a whole
My soul is nothing but the blackness of the walls that surround me
My mind just can't get back from that horrid place
My nightmares are in the walls that only I can see.

If would I still be there would I still be alone
Judging my worth, while all the victims are in me
the death of so many seems the torment of one
there seems no hope for this bloodied mind, but maybe, just maybe,
eventually.

DEAD END

The color of the sky and I,

Dark and gloomy most days long.

Heavy clouds of thunder rippling by,

The stormy heart sings a sour song.

The scent of death still in the air,

Minds all filled with hate.

The myriad of souls are in despair,

For most of us it's just too late.

We line up by two's before the devils den,

All the soldiers of forgotten wars.

Shedding dreams of hopes for when,

Naked hearts abandon to dreadful open sores.

Bleeding eyes and dripping flesh,

Are food for the devil's inn.

What our minds are holding now,

Devour us from within.

Glowing fields of forget-me-nots,

Leading the way to fires of hell.

It's time for the devil to take us,

Now burning deep inside our shell.

Nothing left of life on earth,

The wars have taken toll.

A barren rock in an open sea,

The universe no longer whole.

Man did this his minds of fire,

Challenged his beginning then took his end.

A future no longer a gleaming spire,

The deepest canyons of human mind now too late to mend.

THERE IS HOPE

I can never see beyond the pain
the pain of yesterday and today
the tears and dreams are driving me insane
I can't be happy, there's just no way.

I never imagined seeking help for this
it was something beyond my dreams
the war assaulted me too severe
I'll never know what I have missed.

The beauty, the sparkle, now all behind me
no way now to collect these many treasures
I see no way out except the hanging tree
I now sit alone without any pleasures.

Maybe there's hope but I can't feel my heart
could be I'm dead, have been from the start
now I'll be molded with insanity
my eyes are dead, I may never see.

A glimpse of tiny sparkle came along my path
new friends who wants me to be me
unbinding my heart and clearing my eyes
maybe in the long run they'll help me see.

THE FEAR INSIDE

Are you still afraid of the dark?
is your life still filled with fear?
are your eyes still filled with hate?
do you feel death is all too near?

Is depression your only way of life?
are you letting the rain pass through your eyes?
are the dark rain clouds clogging your brain?
are you still listening to all the lies?

Brighten your life with someone to talk to
listen yourself instead of closing your mind
the monsters in your thoughts have not yet whipped you
There's fight in your heart deep down inside.

Bring out the sword and confront your demons
take the fight to your realm, there's no hope for him there
open your mind and get what's past due
Conquer your fears and brave to be you.

BE GONE

Be gone my hellish nightmares
I'm not back there any more
Trying to start a new existence
With my heart and brain still sore.

Be gone all these insane memories
Life is too short please let me live
Take away the heartache and frustration
The pain I have is just too massive.

Be gone the blackness in my heart
All new blood is rushing in
I can't yet smell the flowers
This life I'm living should be a sin.

Be gone the torment that possesses my soul
I don't have room for you any more
Love's coming in and it's really a blessing
Please let go so I can soar.

DYING TIME

War is an angry dimension
Of souls all bloodied and torn,
Good minds all wasted everyday
And the hometown people mourn.

Intertwined in a memory block
Are scenes from this horrid time,
The illicit odor of dying flesh
And another mountain to climb.

Then roses start to grow now
In all the fields of pain,
Fertilized only by the blood of man
The dead, the wounded and insane.

The dying time is gone for me
But still lingers in my mind,
Fingers of hate behind my eyes
Squeezing nerves throughout they bind.

Now only death will heal
These crazy thoughts in me,
Storming through the waves of war
Blood and death is all I see.

The flowers bloom in that far off land

But when will the roses grow for me,

Upon my death is the likely time

Nurtured and fertilized by only me.

ANOTHER LIFE

Loneliness is a way of life for so many
It seems to justify the existence of anxiety and despair
Depression is prominent, nothing left to hope for
Soon you feel the fear of other people, no one to share.

It leaves you empty, emptier than ever before
There's a whole lot missing in your troubled life
It helps to talk but who wants to hear
The private pain seems to add to all the strife.

It can be beaten, this horrible way of living
I've been through it with help from angels above
They sent me someone who could understand
Someone to talk to, another lonely dove.

I still get depressed, still the weird dreams
Don't get me wrong; it's not an absolute cure
But now I can share, the burden is lighter
My life has improved beyond my past hopes, a lot less to endure.

Someone to talk to, someone to share
Someone to be there when I shed a tear
It is more than I hoped for, the past almost gone
Sharing my life with a special love, now without fear.

FOR MY SINS

The darkness is in me

The blindness is tearing me apart

The emotional hate, the all too present fear

This darkness is destroying my heart

There's a black empty void in my soul

Unspeakable terror surrounds me

My body aches, torment and pain is what I feel

In the bright powerful light of heaven, I'll never see

Then comes the ending, the fires of hell

The devil wants me for his own

My skin starts to peel, the blackness of blood

In the darkness, in the corner, I feel so alone

Everyone else is seeing the light

Oh, God in heaven, what have I done?

I left, I ran, I tried to find oneness

In my selfish quest I abandoned my son

Now the trial is mine, for my own massive sins

I'll never have another chance at this

I belong to the devil, the whole of me

Never to know the eternal bliss

PEACE WILL COME

Are you living with fear in your heart?

Do you feel like freedom is just an illusion?

Are you still trying to reach and feel it's not there?

Is the past still confronting you, the blood and confusion?

Try to relax my friend, you can learn to see.

It's just one more challenge you have to face.

You survived the past, you're almost free.

You can get through it with just one good friend.

Are you still blinded by the fear and the hate?

Are you afraid of the dark and sleepless nights?

Speak to the angels; they'll hear your plea.

Relax your heart, search for the love and brand new heights.

It's a real good climb, but the rewards are there.

The angels will see to that.

Those fearless little angels will show you the way.

Well beyond time, above all the bounds, and plenty to spare.

It's well worth the trip, beyond all your fears.

To be with the angels and all the wonders.

Your heart will absorb, your mind will be free.

Beyond all the torment that put us under.

Your freedom is coming to you, it has with me.

It took years away from my life, but now I can see.

It took a long time, the emotional strife.

But the angels are helping, they sent me a wife.

SOMEWHERE

Somewhere in time there is a peaceful moment,
one with no fear and confusion.
Somewhere out there, there is life to behold,
but what if life itself is just an illusion.

Somewhere in time there's a room without memories,
a safeguard from the errors of war.
There's too much in the distance that needs to be told,
out there past the stars there's so much more.

Somewhere in time a future unfolds,
a place for solitude that only I can share.
To give me the peace and solace I need,
in the far distance of time someone must care.

Somewhere in time is that moment for me,
someday I'll find it then to know what I am.
Rid me of the poison that surrounds my mind,
to cover me with warmth much more than I can.

Somewhere in time is me without past,
Cleansed to the prime the memories are gone.
Living out there could be an illusion too,
I succumb to the heavens, no longer that strong.

SIMPLY LOVE

Love isn't blind; I see it all around me

no pretense, no hostility, no fear

a whole new life has evolved in my soul

with your love in the center I can truly see.

No more complexity, no more confusion

nothing but harmony and honesty rest with me

the surrounding of everything beautiful

the striking colors, the elusive hue's

the lure of your love is in all of me.

BEYOND HOPE

There isn't time to enjoy it all
all the treasure's I see around me
the wonders on all the earth and then the stars and beyond
the heavens and all it covers, too much for one to see.

But it's more than just seeing, you can feel what's around you
feel it in your heart and know that it's there
your soul covers so much more than your lifetime
feel the freedom to see, more than enough to share.

Find your love and open the heavens
enough for two in your travels through time
time itself is a wondrous wonder
not in the clock but your own fearless mind.

Leave the earth and the angels will find you
those heavenly wonders sparkling so bright
you can feel their presence above and beyond
just before you get to the bright white light.

Travel the heavens with these beautiful saviors
they'll enter your soul and take you from there
You're beyond time now, you can feel the freedom
with that love by your side, you'll have nothing to fear.

SEE TO BELIEVE

Are you blind my friend, can't you see?

the wonders of life, the beauty of nature

the trees, the grass, the flowers that be

the oceans abound with living ecstasy.

Beautiful life is all around us

the nature of the soul is of utmost importance

it harbors the kindness and all the love we feel

open your eyes my friend and be one of us.

We can show you the way and you'll never forget

the emptiness will disappear

life's too important to pass all this by

enjoy the wonders, let go your fears.

CHILD OF THE STARS

Only the children of the stars know for sure

The unborn children in our lives

The knowledge they hold, the universal tour

Beyond all limits of time, beyond man's reality

Man could never reach so far as what the unborn know

There <u>are</u> no limits beyond the stars

The unborn children have been there, further than reality.

The unborn children in our lives.

LIFE?

The purpose of this exercise -

To enrich your soul through the comfort and trust of another soul.

To combine together, to strengthen the inner entity with the
same though different of another soul.

To experience the most personal transfer of wisdom and caring.

To develop to the strongest possible all encompassing oneness
with the total freedom to love without reason.

An incredulous, seemingly boundless journey….. to the beginning.

CHANGING

Now I have a goal and now the race is on
The tears are drying up, the walls are coming down
Tiny particles of light are working their way in
Slowly devouring the blackness and all the pain within.

The future is forever now, forever I will see
Across the mass of land and over the trembling sea
Everything's so beautiful now and colors all abound
I found a whole new strength in me, now love is all around.

I can feel the warmth rushing in, caressing every cell
Out of the darkness, out of the fire and out of the clutches of hell
A forever love is with me now, forever and a day
Till death do us part I have proclaimed, peace is now my way.

Multitudes of flecks of light are stampeding through my eyes
A whole new world is open to me, a world where no one dies
Life is at a new beginning, love is here to stay
I've seen the death; I've seen the war, way behind me on this day.

Many happy days ahead, promised by the vows I took
Beauty is now a way of life, I've opened my eyes to look
I can see all the flowers now, stretching toward the big blue sky
Nothing in my world but peace, this love will never die.

ETERNAL

The war is far behind me now

I found someone to talk to

I found someone to hold my hand

My darling angel, you know it's you.

The flowers I send, the sparkle in my eyes

Lets everyone know I care

It's free to see these gifts of love

I'll be with you forever, forever these eternal ties.

The seeds of love are well within

They're growing continuously through my heart

Day after day I feel more alive

I knew you'd be with me right from the start.

You're the one I needed through all my trying years

And you're still with me, my thanks to the heavens

That's where you came from to help with my tears

I can feel your soft wings gathering up my demons.

STAY AWHILE

Stay awhile with me, help me understand
help me see the bright new colors - in all this wonderland
a counsel for my weathered mind, a shoulder to ease the pain
a welcome smile, a gentle touch and I'll be in the promise lane.

Stay awhile with me, see me through the night
waken me if I should shake, hold on tight if I should fright
listen to my dreams and hug me if I shed a tear
be with me if I start to quiver, let me know that you're still near.

Stay awhile with me, my love is always standing by
we'll start new memories every day, then see if we can fly
hold my hand if the need arises, hold me, hold me with all your might
nothing dearer in this life than you in that soft white light.

Stay awhile with me, nothing more to fear
with you now by my side, I may no longer have that tear
life is easing up on me, nothing I can't do
as long as we're together, everything on earth is new.

Stay awhile with me, the promises I'll never break

your love is in me, mine in you, right now and forever as long as it

should take

the heavens are on our side now, the prayers are now in place

for together we'll go to the promised land, now there's nothing we

can't face.

FOR MY LOVE

I'm as happy as I'll ever be
I have a wife now who really loves me.
The love I feel will never end
Everything is open, nothing to defend.

Valentine's day was a miracle to me
Everything from that day on.
There was nothing more spectacular to see
I have it all absorbed in my heart.

No more fears and no more tears
No more loneliness beyond my years.
I feel a wholeness I never had
I'll never again feel that sad.

Thank you my darling for all your love
Sweeter than a pure white dove.
You're with me forever and so complete
I still send you flowers with no one to compete.

You're in my heart for now and forever
Worry not my love, I'll leave you never.
I'll always see the best in you
The holding hands I'll never sever.

HOLDING ON

Hold on to me my precious love

Wrap your arms around me tight

The twinkling stars are just above

Hold me tight enough, we both may see the light.

I need your love for my entire being

Together we can stretch to the open sea

Just hold on long enough, we can make it

Don't ever let go for I'll lose what is me.

Hold on to me my loving wife

I really need what you came to offer

I'll hold it deep and deeper still

Just hold me tight; we'll share each other.

Together is the only way it should be

Apart we're each no longer a one

You will never be tried or alone

Hold on to me my previous love.

MY DARLING

Come to me my darling angel
hold me and love me with all your heart
cherish the moments we have to share
with caring and compassion right from the start.

I know your love, it's really a treasure
I feel it every day and far into the night
you're in my dreams, in my every thought
so much love, so much of a wondrous pleasure.

Your wholesome goodness, just one of a kind
you're thoughtful whispers, I know you're mine
I can trust you with my deepest worries
you're the only loving angel in my mind.

MY WIFE

In the presence of my lovely wife
The loneliness is gone, the heartache whisked away
I feel more alive than all the whole of my former life
A new existence is here, now and forever to stay

An enormous presence sent me a miracle to cherish
The angels look upon me in wonder
My new wife came from far off in a dream
Just a dream that put me in the spell I'm under

The gentle kisses, the quiet talks
The looks of love, the calm slow walks
A perfect togetherness, everything to share
The harmony of doves, the sharing of care

No longer alone to search for the stars
A partner so loving that shares my soul
Together we can reach the farthest star
Where the alabaster angels, in wonder, accept our toll

It will last forever, this wholesome love
Forever and a day we'll stay
For now I can see the path ahead
Clean, bright, forever beautiful along the way

MY LOVE

The Universe is all around us
an immense space without time
filled with a myriad of bright little angels
not one brighter than mine.

She's in my mind and deep in my heart
she's flooded my soul with light
she's everywhere I could possibly be
far past the stars and still brightens my night.

She came to me late, in my waning years
she came to me from a dream I had
she opened my mind and gave me new life
she gave me reason to be and wiped away my tears
this angel that came to me, now my beautiful wife.

ONCE IN A LIFETIME

Only once in a lifetime, comes a very special angel,

so warm and gentle and full of love as with all the heavens.

The stars shine brighter, the moon stays full

and the heart is swollen twice the size.

An angel to make the past remote,

the present alive and the future full of hope.

A chance to go beyond simple reason,

the hearts coming together and the souls joining in

such a warmth that all life revolves around them.

A chance to make this once in a lifetime

a complete future for two.

A part of life, but above and beyond the basic pleasures.

A complete gift to each other, the feel of another heart,

so close, so within, that the stars are in envy.

Two souls that would make it past the end

into the true fullness of existence.

Only once in a lifetime.

ANGELS ABOVE

Clean as a bell these little angels
An iridescent sparkling form for all.
Peace and tranquility they try to pass
As they cherish all the souls below.

Then we ignore them, these shiny wonders
Trying to justify our sour lives and still stand tall.
Almost unknown are these glimpses of sparkle
They go unobserved and unheard by all.

These bright little angels travel the heavens
Searching for souls to pass the word.
The heavens are closing all around us
And the only acknowledge is fear and the sword.

There is still time if we learn to listen
No one needs shed a tear.
The angels are out there and so very near
And still we stand and challenge our very soul.

Remember your soul; open it up,
and soon you'll know
The angels themselves are there for us.
These bright little angels for all to trust.

ANGELS IN OUR LIVES

The angels have all come down to hold me
They're entwined in my heart and my very soul
I'm far away from the years of war
I'm far away from the pain and fear that held me.

I'm on my way to a joyous life; I have the angels to hold my hand
They take me far away, past the void and into the light
Outside the crucible of life, beyond my sins so rife
The angels are with me, a miracle glow that shines through the night.

The angles don't know the boundaries of time; they were here long
before us
The angels are all around us, open your heart to enjoy
The miracle's they pass along, the endless love they give us
They get in our soul and make us believe, and then they just surround us.

You can see them with your heart from far off in the distance
They're in all our minds encompassing our very existence
They know no boundaries, no limits to defend
They're in the unborn from beginning to end.

They give us the love we share with each other
They give us the kindness that gives us our wealth
The angels themselves are the catalyst
For that which creates love and life itself.

NOTHING BUT LOVE

The atoms of love in my heart
out number the fish in the sea
There is no end to my loving you
I'll be here for all eternity.

My love is more powerful than the oceans
I'll climb the highest mountain to get to your heart
I'll walk through hell if that's what it takes
together we can make a brand new start.

When I first laid eyes on you, it took by breath away
I smiled in wonder at what I'd seen
your compassion, your grace, your open soul
to comfort me and plant a seed.

Now we can walk on the ocean
for God and all to see
the seed has grown to enormous depths
far deeper than the deepest blue sea.

I cherish your love like nothing else
I'll keep it into a second life
I'll hold on to you far past existence
to hold, to comfort, for now you're my wife.

THE END

Still the deep depression, thoughts of my own death
Still the sleepless nights, no comfort in my bed
Still the feeling I don't belong, after all these years of help
Still the lifelong battle, the fight that takes my breath

Still pushing people away, the friends I'll never have
That Vietnam is always there, at night I go to hell
I thought I'd reached a compromise, but all to no avail
It's still within me, all the demons; death is at the ready for that one
last rusty nail

Post traumatic stress they call it, in me, a life long threat
I feel I'm going backwards, the anger comes in waves
Sleepless nights, the taunting dreams, still the feeling of insane
A never ending battle, thoughts of suicide now a game

So many years of fighting this, I fear I've lost my will
Death itself means nothing, the demons in me still
The marriage I'm in, the love I feel, doesn't dismiss my sins
Depression getting the better of me, the devil always wins

This poem is at the end to show there's no respite
It's always there, this life long battle, in me and by myself
Nothing more to write now, all is said and done
I love my wife, she's all I have, but those fires of hell have surely won

PEACE AGAIN

Many days have passed now
My wife is holding tight
I realize now I'm not alone
To stand alone through another fight

She shares my burden and lightens my load
The help I sought is next to me
That devil is losing his grip again
Just another nightmare, with my wife to help me see

Another day gone by, the sky now getting brighter
Depression easing up again, no longer in that fire
The fragrance of the flowers around me cast a gentle spell
My wife is by my side again, her love will never tire

All it takes is someone to hold
Someone who cares and understands
To help me through the toughest nights
To help me through the pain of the fiery drifting sands

Someone to cry with me and ease my troubled mind
Someone to hold my hand and talk me through the hell
Someone to be there just to share the burning horror
Someone to hold the door while I walk out of my shell

JUST A WHISPER

Just a whisper of my angel's wings

tells me life is new again

the gentle surf on the ocean shore

lets me know its time to begin.

Among the whispers of the soft green leaves

to the flowers swaying to and fro

the silent whisper of the butterfly

tells me what I need to know.

The gentle breeze of the humming bird

the kissable sign of the morning dew

just a whisper will change my life

lets each day begin anew.

BATTLE OF GOOD FRIDAY

From the after action report:

On Thursday, April 11, 1968 the 3rd Battalion, 22nd Infantry, of the 25th infantry, acting on reports of intensive enemy activity, climbed from choppers into a remote jungle area 13 miles north of the Dau Tieng base camp. In the few hours before darkness the Regulars busied themselves by establishing a perimeter of hastily prepared foxholes. As darkness quickly surrounded them, they made themselves as comfortable as possible.

At twenty minutes past four o'clock on a black Good Friday morning, all hell broke loose.

Companies B, C, and D, of the 3rd Battalion, 22nd Infantry had "combat assaulted," into the area designated and carefully swept the outskirts before establishing three ambush patrols and three listening posts. The larger position was arranged in a clearing surrounded by jungle, ranging from single to triple canopy. Scattered trees and anthills caused some obstruction, however, the flat terrain provided good fields of fire.

The Battalion Commander employed the three companies on the defensive perimeter, holding the Reconnaissance Platoon as a reserve. All elements were arranged to employ interlocking fires.

At approximately 0230 hours on 12 April 1968, Good Friday, the perimeter received light probing fire from the west. The Regulars answered it with small arms, automatic weapons and Claymore mines.

Between 0330 and 0400 hours, the enemy launched a heavy and accurate mortar attack on the perimeter using 61 and 82 millimeter mortars. Approximately 125 rounds landed inside the perimeter, causing numerous casualties.

The mortar barrage reached peak intensity at about 0405 hours and a massive ground attack followed. Charlie Company held the right flank and Delta the left. Using small arms, automatic weapons, 90mm recoilless rifles, hand grenades and bayonets, the Infantrymen repulsed the enemy as fast as they came on. As the attack grew more intense, artillery support was called in and it arrived quickly.

Launching more and more "human wave" assaults, the enemy penetrated the defensive line. Bravo Company was forced to pull back approximately 50 meters as they were being overrun. Elements from the Recon Platoon and Delta Company moved across the beaten zone to reinforce Bravo and deliver ammunition. Charlie Company turned its left flank machine guns upon the advancing enemy as they streamed across Bravo's bunkers. This crossfire caught the enemy in a vice between Delta and Charlie Companies, as reinforced Bravo Company fought its way back to the main bunker line.

Combined with tactical air strikes, gunships, artillery and the fast approach of the 2ⁿᵈ Battalion, 22ⁿᵈ Infantry (Mechanized), the foot soldiers of the 3ʳᵈ Battalion repulsed the enemy and the perimeter was secured by 0630 hours.

Fighting had been extremely fierce during the push to regain the bunker line. Some of the enemy died at a range of 5 meters and in some instances, hand to hand combat occurred. 127 enemy died within the perimeter.

As morning light appeared, the 2ⁿᵈ Battalion, 22ⁿᵈ Infantry (Mechanized) merged into the 3ʳᵈ Battalion's perimeter to reinforce. They had battled pockets of resistance through five miles of jungle, at night, to get to their American counterparts.

As the Commander of Charlie Company, 2/22 Infantry and his mechanized troopers approached firing their fifty calibers, the enemy fled west into the jungle. All contact was broken by 0730 hours. The enemy left behind 153 bodies along with a substantial amount of equipment.

At 0800 hours, 12 April 1968, The Brigadier General, Assistant Division Commander of the 25ᵗʰ Infantry Division arrived to survey the battlefield and present awards.

The following statistical data was submitted shortly after the battle:

(1) 16 US Killed in Action. 47 Wounded.

(2) 153 enemy Killed in Action, 53 additional reported forward of the perimeter by aerial summary and recon patrols.

(3) Weapons and equipment captured:

> 45 AK-47 Assault Rifles
> 7 AK-50 Assault Rifles
> 13 Light Machine Guns
> 7 RPG-2 Rocket Launchers
> 2 Bold Action Carbines
> 38 RPG-2 Rounds
> 5 RPG-7 Rounds
> 93 Hand Grenades
> 29 Light Machine Gun Ammo Drums

The 25th division departed the perimeter on the following morning after burying the dead and policing the battlefield. They spent Easter Sunday at their Base Camp, Dau Tieng.

ONE WAY OUT

The wars, the hate, the cruelty abound, tortured minds across the lands

It's a frightening place to be, the only home that we call earth

Is it insanity that's taken hold; is isolation the only cure?

The hate, the fears, the broken souls, will insanity be inbred in

every birth?

The black empty walls surround me, only the medals of long ago

All alone with tears for the dead, all the wounded and insane

No family, no friends, is the way it has to be

Isolation is what I crave; my way of life has left me inane

I've had my war, I've had my hate, and I've given cruelty along the way

Medals from the war all I've thrown away, nothing left save all the fear

Isolation was all I wanted, to hide all the tears and confusion

But after many years, an angel came, and she wiped away a tear

I used to wake with screams from my heart; for my heart was a

lonely place to be

No one entered, no one shared, it was a dark morbid place for only me

But now the flowery scent of love is pushing it's way in

Now I feel a new beginning, my heart is warming up, right now, a

worthwhile place to be

The pain still there; the tears still come and go, but now I have

some peace within

With that little angel next to me I no longer have to hide

The torture in my mind, giving way to a startling new beginning

Away from the war and confusion, now someone by my side

Now I can hear the ocean waves and see the stars at night

The angels flickering all around absorbing all my fright

Life is easing up on me, a whole new place to be

The tears I've had alone are easing up, for my love is holding tight

News Clippings about the battle:

From the Pacific Stars and Stripes:

Headline: GI's smash Red Attack.

Saigon (AP) fighting from foxholes at a range of a few feet, American infantrymen repulsed 400 newly equipped enemy troops who stormed U.S. positions early Friday in War Zone C, 49 miles northwest of Saigon.

After five hours of close-quarter fighting, the North Vietnamese and Viet Cong attackers fled, leaving 128 dead and more than 50 weapons on the Battlefield. All the enemy dead were killed inside or on the fringes of the U. S. Perimeter & 16 U.S. troops were killed and 47 wounded. Associated Press photographer Al Chang reported from the battlefield that the fighting was so close at one point the American Infantrymen fixed their bayonets for hand-to-hand fighting as their ammunition got low. They didn't have to use them. *(See following note about the use of bayonets at Good Friday).*

Two American Infantrymen were found dead inside their bunker. Around them were eight Viet Cong troops, gunned down by the two before they were killed. A lone radio operator held out against ten Viet Cong until the Company Commander, and three Infantrymen reinforced him.

A wounded North Vietnamese prisoner identified his unit as the 245th Battalion of the 271st Viet Cong Main Force Regiment.

(Note: Perplexed by Mr. Al Chang's comment that bayonets were fixed but not used, it was explained to this writer that it was policy to never admit that American Infantrymen had run so low on ammunition that they were forced to use bayonets. However, the two Bravo Company soldiers that gave their lives while taking out eight NVA, had bayonets on their rifles with blood on them. The enemy dead had bayonet holes in them. The American rifles and magazines were empty.)

Excerpt from The Santa Cruz Sentinel (California)

Headline: Every Man A Hero As Reds Hit Line.

Commander of the Company that was one of the hardest hit said: "When I heard the small-arms fire then I knew it was a ground attack. Five minutes later, my front lines facing the thick, heavy jungle opened up. From then on it was a lot of shooting."

Commander of another company said: "The attack pushed into the area of my First Platoon and before long they had only one man left. The Second Platoon was in danger of being overrun and I pulled it back about twenty yards and from there it held."

A platoon sergeant said, "I retook a position with four men in my squad right after daybreak so I could see where the Viet Cong were. He found himself out of ammunition, picked up an enemy rifle, and killed two Viet Cong. He was one of those receiving the Silver Star, but said he didn't know why he got it.

The Lieutenant Colonel summing up the battle said: "I had a lot of heroes in my battalion. I wish the Americans back home could appreciate the Americans here the way I do. I've got a lot of real heroes here. You can't find better men than that."

This writer remembers . . . . .

We flew into the clearing late on the afternoon of 11 April 1968. We were delayed getting out of our pick up zone due to a shortage of choppers. A major operation was underway and aircraft were in short supply. The last unit reached the clearing at about 1700 hours. By the time listening posts, patrols and the defensive line were established, it was almost dark.

Charlie Company was the first to arrive and consequently had more time to dig in. Bravo came in last and faced the task of preparing their positions in dim light. The ground was as hard as a rock and entrenching tool tips were blunted trying to get dug in.

The battalion was postured facing west. Bravo Company had the center; Charlie was on the right, looking west and north, while Delta had the left, facing southwest. The perimeter was arranged in an arc or semi-circle. Recon Platoon covered the rear.

Normal actions for a defense were accomplished such as LP's, trip flares, listening devices, etc., but it was difficult trying to clear fields of fire or string barbed wire in the dark. The Charlie and Bravo Company Commanders met at their tie in point and fortunately, there appeared an ideal situation for placing two of Charlie Company's M-60 machine guns in pairs, their fields of fire grazing across the front of Bravo. Those two guns were able to place grazing fire across the enemy's penetration into Bravo later that night. Both commanders' were deeply concerned that such little preparation had been accomplished before darkness. They still had rations and water to distribute among the myriad of things required in a defense. Bravo Company men had barely scratched the surface of the cast iron earth before darkness arrived.

Enemy mortars initiated the attack and it wasn't long before the battlefield was a sea of green tracers. They cut so low you couldn't get your head up. In minutes they were pouring right through Bravo's positions. Charlie Company was also heavily engaged but the fact that they had holes to fight from saved them from being overrun. Charlie Company counted 56 bodies laying in front of their positions at daylight.

Delta Company had an ambush patrol stuck out in the jungle between the enemy and their positions. They couldn't get back in. Delta was also hit hard and soon they were all isolated pockets of resistance.

It didn't take long to conclude that the main thrust was through Bravo. The Colonel was quick to arrange support and within seconds artillery was falling to the front. The Lieutenant of Charlie Company Forward Observer and the Battalion Artillery Liaison Officer from the 2nd Battalion, 77th Field Artillery had laid in defensive concentrations close to our perimeter. They continued to direct it throughout the battle.

A gunship from the 188th Assault Helicopter Company arrived overhead and their red tracers hosed down our front. Soon other gunships arrived from the 116th AHC the 187th. Those brave guys were always there for us. "Spooky," a modified C-47 airplane came overhead and poured all his firepower forward of the perimeter. Air Force fighter-bombers came on station and dropped their napalm canisters and bombs as close as fifty meters in front of our lines. The battlefield was a sea of flame, red and green tracers, and white-hot steal from the artillery.

Knowing that the 2nd Battalion, 22nd Infantry (Mechanized) was fast approaching from the southeast, the 25th div. (the regulars) took heart and met the enemy head on, bullet for bullet, bayonet for bayonet. Charlie Company reacted to enemy troops on top of the Battalion Commanders CP. After they eliminated that threat, they gathered up a couple of men, and with machine guns and rifles blazing, they made their way into the center of Bravo's line. They had the enemy in a cross fire between them and Delta and what was left of Bravo. This combined effort all together killed 127 enemies between Bravo's line and about 75 feet to the rear of it.

Delta Company boys brought in ammunition, distributed it and fought the attacking enemy at the same time.

Whatever medals and accolades those fellows got that night, they darned sure deserved them.

By daylight the mechanized infantry had arrived. They were reconing by fire and their big fifty's were beginning to hit inside our perimeter. The first track to arrive and its gunner, called for a cease-fire as soon as they broke through. At the Gettysburg reunion for the 22nd Infantry last October, a veteran of that unit told me he stopped firing because all he could see were Americans and Viet Cong merged together on the battlefield. "I didn't know who to shoot at," he said.

By 0800 hours we were stacking the dead. We had to pack dirt into the wounds of some of them to stop the smoldering napalm from consuming their flesh. The Brigade Chaplain arrived and began to anoint the 16 Americans and pray for them. He told me he was also praying for the North Vietnamese and Viet Cong dead. Let me leave it at that.

This Easter season, let us all remember the 16 brave Americans that gave their lives in that jungle clearing that terrible night. Let's remember the wounded, some of them amputees, today. Oh yes, as the chaplain would have it, let's remember also, the enemy that we killed and wounded thirty years ago this week. As he told me once, there is an old Russian saying: "The only thing different between soldiers is the buttons on their uniforms."

Contents

Notes

Notes

Notes

ORDER BLANK

To order an additional copy of

Images From Hell

please send $11.45
plus $2.50 for shipping and handling to:

F. L. RIKER
P. O. Box 642
Youngtown, AZ 85363

If you have internet access,
visit my web site at:

imagesfromhell.com

Please send me _____ books @ $11.45 each *(please add $2.50 to cover shipping and handling for each book ordered to a maximum of $5.00).* I am enclosing $_____

   I would like an autographed copy *(please indicate the name of the recipient).*

_____

Name _____

Address _____

City _____ State/Zip _____

Send check or money order – *no cash or C.O.D.'s please. Prices are subject to change without notice. Please allow four to six weeks for delivery.*

ABOUT THE AUTHOR

F. L. Riker was just like many of the men who went to serve his country during the Vietnam War. He knew he was doing the right thing to help protect the nation that he loved. But, like many others at his young age, he was not prepared for what he would encounter there. One day he was a civilian, enjoying life in the U.S., and the next day, he was a soldier in a war thousands of miles from home.

When it was all over, Frank returned to an unfriendly country, the United States, where, after many tormented years he was diagnosed with Post-Traumatic Stress Disorder (P.T.S.D.), a mental and emotional ailment that makes him feel he is all alone and has no one to rely on for understanding and support. The circumstances of the war continue to play inside his mind. To help cleanse these feelings, he just completed writing his first book "Images From Hell" in verse, in which he tells his personal story, words from the darkest corners of his mind, from start to finish, so that readers can understand what he and thousands of other soldiers have gone through. He is now starting to write his autobiography about his tormenting years of living with P.T.S.D.

Frank's touching verses shed light on his wartime experiences. His poems include *Alone, The Effect of War, One Fight, Isolation, Savage Country, The Fear Inside* and many more. Readers are able to follow his journey from the depths of despair to finding love, though the horrors and nightmares still emerge from time to time. Veterans are able to understand not only Frank's feelings, but their own, in a fresh new light, and can now have the courage to face their demons as well.

CPSIA information can be obtained
at www.ICGtesting.com
Printed in the USA
FSOW01n0318050115
4315FS

9 781420 842852